Diary of a Langford Girl

Copyright © Jennifer Jenkins 2019

KDP & Alice Drake Publishing
Toronto, Ontario Canada

Cover Art Design/ Original Artwork © Jenn Zed 2019
Ink and Watercolour
United Kingdom

Photography © Jennifer Jenkins (unless stated otherwise)

ISBN 978-1-72715-680-5

Contents

Acknowledgements

Heartfelt gratitude to my beloved west coast family and friends for making my long overdue visit so memorable; thank you for Langfordpalooza, family time, fishing, beer, so many laughs and old-time recaps. Love to you all.

A very gracious thank you to poet and artist, Jenn Zed, for capturing my vision so poignantly in her cover art. I'm honoured by your collaboration.

To my daughter, Chloe, for helping me funnel my thoughts during all the hours I spent burning the wick; thank you for your ongoing encouragement and support, and for your amazing eye for style and detail; I love you.

Lastly, to all who contributed to my memories and inspiration even if you didn't know you did; thank you.

Introduction

It was a blazing hot August when I returned from the island; the manic high of my visit still running rampant through my blood, the lusty tail of summer wagging like a metronome as I sat outside with my notebook writing fervently until the sun lowered; the smell of smoke and the sea, still lingering on my skin, my clothes, my hair…

Thought-bubbles burst from a vessel; ink-stained and isolated, enunciated by nothing; the breeze, rootless, gibberish, a dreamer's language. Days seemed to end and begin as though the day I left, began and never ended; twenty-five years trying to explain my heart— and while there's a chance none of it will make sense, there is always hope; hope of reuniting, of reincarnation; hope that the wistful undertone of memories will remind us how we used to be.

The Jellyfish Backstory

There is something inherently magical about being born and raised on Vancouver Island, just as there is something plainly haunting about leaving it. From the mountains and the ocean, the rainforests and wildflowers, to the fog and blazing bulbs of sunset, it is the picture-perfect setting for a child to grow up full of wonder and awe.

More than just a birthplace or a home, the island is an entity, an extension of self; a vessel of spirit. Leaving it behind when I moved to Ontario as a teenager felt much like a sinking ship. I said goodbye to everything I knew and loved: my extended family, my boyfriend, my friends, my cats, my father and the island itself. The feelings associated with such uprooting are abysmal and complex, but aside from the boring self indulgence of personal wounding, there is simply a deep unspoken draw from the island that makes it difficult to forget or leave behind.

I went back for that sunken ship several years later, but it was full of holes and ghosts. I held that long lash of kelp in my hands again as if it were the island's umbilical cord pulling me back into the sea; it hurled my body against the waves and rinsed my heart clean before the tide tossed me out and back to shore. And while it felt very healing at the time, it didn't last. There was no ship. I was the ship; I just didn't know it at the time.

I was happy to be home, but my heart was fractured; I became terribly homesick for my mother and siblings, and a few years later, I returned to Ontario. I went to college, started a family of my own, and I've been sailing the eastern time zone ever since. And while I don't entirely regret leaving Victoria a second time, (I have a wonderful son and a beautiful daughter as a result), it's probably safe to say that I'll be plotting my escape back to the island for the rest of my life.

I grew up in Langford; a town once considered the middle of nowhere and the ghetto of Vancouver Island. An infamous sort of town with a rough, redneck reputation, a town that coined its own phrases and dress code; it even had its own nicknames. The Olde Country, as it is sometimes affectionately known, or the Dogpatch or Langhole when there were no jobs or sidewalks or streetlights.

It was the 80's and most of us were poor, but we were hearty kids, content with peanut butter sandwiches and hotdogs wrapped in white bread, and when we needed money, we collected empties at 10 cents a pop. We didn't stay inside, (or at home), unless we had a fort, an ant hill to blow up, or a stack of mint aeros to melt in the microwave. We walked, biked, hitchhiked or rode in rusty shopping carts when we wanted to meet friends, go for a swim at the lake, find a party, a bootlegger, a smoke...anything. We were born in a time when coming of age was ripe with danger; tameless and unrestrained as we forged through fields of wet leather, the first taste of flesh, hard liquor and metal; it was a visceral age of rare freedom when our world was unbridled, overlooked and underdeveloped.

Langford was lord of the loitering asshole, bringing droves of kids to the heart of town on Goldstream Avenue. The 7-11, Western Foods plaza and John's Arcade were common hotspots where everyone congregated on Friday nights— and there, nestled in the coattails of skid row, sat the notorious Westwind Pub where our parents and older siblings set the stage for what was inevitably to come. We terrorised the sub shop and the Night Owl (a convenience store that my friends robbed every weekend) and spent endless nights in Hall's Field where we picked magic mushrooms and passed out in the blackberries after too much drinking.

You get the picture, Langford was a teenager's glory with plenty of places to be bad, and if you ever hear someone say, "that's so Langford", you'll know it means "that's so ghetto".

Aside from the plethora of blatant alcoholics, potheads, petty thieves and exaggerated squalor, Langford was a beautiful place to live. Nostalgic and quaint with a railroad that crossed through town, when folks still travelled the Dayliner with their umbrellas and ordinary brown suitcases, and long before that, day-trippers came by diesel railcar during the gold rush in the mid 1800's.

There was no gold rush in the 80's that's for sure, but the train tracks still led to some rich places that entertained the imagination, including an old gold mine with moss-covered tunnels and heaps of hanging lichen. It was a perilous journey along the tracks at times, looking for dead bodies or bigfoot, or a good place to smoke some homegrown— oh right, *aside f*rom the hoodlums…

I loved being an island girl; in my soul, I have known nothing else. With plenty of open green space, meandering rivers that meet the sea, 600-year-old Douglas firs, mountains and trestles with heights to climb and peaks to conquer that overlook the island's wonder. With the thick, mossy oasis of Goldstream Park where salmon spawn in the fall, and the Esquimalt Lagoon, resurrecting memories of childhood walks with an old English sheepdog, or the love-drunk teenagers making out in a fortress made of driftwood— one of the most tranquil places I've ever known, where sea-air fills your nostrils and freightliners laze on the horizon while beautiful migratory birds bask in the shallows.

The island, still lined with miles of blackberry bramble and the litter of arbutus leaves, make every winding road seem like a time warp; when we were young and tender, when our world was governed by nothing more than nature or the weather. My visit home last summer was deeply reminiscent of these things, despite the smoke from the forest fires that steeped my eyes and stifled my views when the wind blew just right. It was incredibly moving to see my beloved childhood wonders again, and to be embraced by friends and family with so much love you'd never know I'd been gone twenty years. But goddamn they warned me, they said everything had changed, that I wouldn't recognise this town, and they were right.

I'd been back to the island with my children nine years prior, but we were only there for a few days, and they were very sad circumstances as my Grandmother had passed away. Langford was undergoing the initial onset of its transformation then, with the collapse of the railway and the massive erection of the iron arch that read "Welcome to Goldstream Village", and while I rolled my eyes at the atrocity, I was relieved to see the rest of our town looking relatively the same. I hadn't been home in 15 years at that point, but I still got around just fine; I never needed a map on the island, not ever.

This time around it was as if I'd never set foot in Langford in all my life; our imprints had been erased. It felt like a masquerade ball where people seemed strangely familiar, but the knowing was so hidden beneath the costume that I couldn't decipher what I was looking at. I didn't mean to cry, but there I was driving around in my rental car with some digital ho telling me to turn down streets I'd never heard of before, when all the streets I did know came to a dead end. Remember when Alice cried those gigantic tears somewhere in Wonderland because the key wouldn't fit in the door and she couldn't find her way home? It was like that.

I was shocked to see my underdeveloped, heavy-metal universe built up into a fluffy, pretentious, super-glam metropolis with a Starbucks on every corner. I was overwhelmed with new subdivisions, Costco, condos, restaurants, rec centres, overpasses, rushing-buzzing-honking bewilderment, and I was disoriented and confused when I nearly crashed into a water fountain surrounded by flowers in the middle of a fucking roundabout on Goldstream Avenue. A water fountain in Langford? The last time I felt that kind of disappointment was when Metallica sold out with the Black album in '91.

I searched high and low for landmarks, for any signs of the ghetto, but all that remained were my schools, my house and a handful of rednecks I went to school with; some forty-something men drinking beer all afternoon while they sat in the front yard of a house; a house that should've been condemned years ago when the centipedes first started making their way through the cracks in the sink tiles, but there it stood in all its dilapidated splendour, directly across the street from a swanky lawyer's office. It was as if I'd been plucked into a scene from the Outsiders, though those boys weren't fifteen and bleeding anymore, they were still Langford Greasers— rugged and handsome, a bit dirty, drinking in the sun, all day long.

Indeed, Langford sold out; a gateway for yuppies who sailed the far seas just to sink their teeth into its shiny new vibe. I suppose these things are inevitable, and it is wonderful that such a lowly little town turned upscale and prosperous for the new generation, to offer jobs and a reputation to be proud of, but Langford newbies don't get it; it's not in their blood, they don't have roots or loyalty and neither did those Black album fans.

I'll admit, it hurts a little knowing that Langford is one of the fastest growing cities in the nation, and though I'm not poor like I was in the 80's, it's so swank I can't even afford to live there now. It pains me that most of what we grew up with is now gone, but the worst part is that it's swarming with pencil-legged indie hipsters drinking $12 soy lattes under the hanging baskets of our old bootleg grounds, and I'm the fucking tourist? Well I'll show them how it really is; I'll jump into that stupid water fountain and cause a ruckus. I will.

Aside from my heartache over new Langford, the feeling of home and the sense of belonging filled me with a love and inspiration I hadn't felt in a very long time. I didn't want to leave, so I had to take everything I wanted back to Ontario with me, everything but the everything else I wanted (which is pretty much everything) so, bags of sticks and rocks, dirt and seashells would have to do. As I reflected on my journey, (shamelessly licking the rocks stuffed in my pockets and rinsing my tongue with beer), I had an epiphany.

I had a story that begged to be told, and without any warning or premeditated thought, words began to burst like birds hatching from my throat, taking little bites out of me, forcing my hand into the inkwell. The need to write was urgent, and I surrendered to it; I wrote into the fall and through the long, hellish Ontario winter; and yes, I went mad, many, many times. This is how it is when you grow up in Langford; this is what you get— a confessional mess of innocence and loss; this thing of expression that lurks inside; this romantic, obsessive, addictive, euphoric, rage-inducing work of angst, joy, heartache and bliss.

For my soul
my mother
my sisters and brother

For the drunks and the stoners
the hooligans and hosers

For my Langford family
with love.

Yesterday on Planet Caravan

when the movers arrived, I left everything;
hopped into the station wagon and gazed out the back
until you disappeared.

I rolled down the window, spat into the wind
and boarded a plane not knowing
where it would land.

when I was homesick, I'd think of the fair
how you put your arm around me and vomited
over the picnic table; how we shuffled October
under our feet, flipping fingers at the shiny
brass school bus.

we discovered a planet called Caravan
our limbs rooting in the hills, in the comfort of leaves
and moss cushioning;
shyness peeled and confused elbows tangled
the moon's cycloptic eye staring down on us—

stars swam to the surface of that black-lit sky
and sank when I took my eyes off you.

I know I said goodbye before the movers came.
that day the sun rose like the dead
and burned my heart to the ground.

Inward Bear

white teddy sat on a shelf all these years.
strong silent type watching as I became a woman.
sometimes I would look at him and wonder
about the girl I used to be:

fifteen
drunk on love
the first time I uncovered my body.

my boyfriend gave me that bear on Valentine's Day
and soon after, I was sent away.
I never mourned a death before, but leaving my life behind
was good practice.

a fire grew slowly and the changes came suddenly.
after some time, I buried that bear in a box,
but every so often we'd ship off again and I'd repack him
giving a sad inward glance as he'd look at me longingly.

I used to have things like notes and photographs
but every move was like a house burning down.

that bear was the only thing that survived my youth;
memories tucked away inside his small
bloated belly

today it finally exploded.

I MET MY FIRST BOYFRIEND at Spencer high school when I was in grade 8, but he wasn't my boyfriend yet. He was picking on my brother's best friend by the Spencer townhouses and I didn't like it, so I busted through the crowd and walked right up to him, shook my fist and said, *"you leave him alone you big bully!"*.

We crossed paths again the following year at Luxton Fair; it was a warm early fall evening and I was guzzling Rockaberry cooler with my friends (underage drinking was normal). I was sitting at the picnic table when he stumbled over and sat down beside me. He was having difficulty sitting up straight as he was drunk and had been riding the Hurricane. I put my arm around him to hold him steady, but his head lolled back and forth, then he lurched over the table and threw up. I leaned over to check if his hair was getting in his mouth, but it didn't move at all; it was feathered perfectly still and lacquered stiff with hairspray. I just stroked the back of his head and told him he'd be ok. That was the only time he ever let me touch his hair. I can still smell the scent of Final Net when I think of him.

When he regained his sense of gravity, he smiled, wiped his mouth on his sleeve and lowered his head to my shoulder. He stayed there for what seemed like hours, and hours turned into days, then months... we were together until the day I moved away, though I don't know how we did because we scrapped like two cats, eating each other up until only our tails were left.

Sabbath Days Revisited

I never went to church
but I still woke up in heaven.
I didn't fear the Gods.

I fell in love with the devil
all legion and hell, a crow in the courtyard
a wizard weaving a spell.

he was a beast in black
his biceps bulging through duct tape
as he bellowed on-stage
Neon Knights holy and bright
I swear that was the song.

I gushed in the crowd
teenage lust eating my oxygen
can't remember when I came so close to love.

I used to play the ouija board
just to see if we'd be together forever;
it always said yes.

the dead are a bunch of lying assholes.

Punk Balloon

when I was sixteen I discovered a punk band
and imagined being opposite stage

faceless
effacing myself in the crowd
in a cloud of smoke.

I was misplaced in those days, lost in the four winds
like a balloon that slipped through your fingers.

I didn't know you became a punk star
but I saw you once, years later—

I stood before you, my guts contorting
like a miserable baby.
everything sank out of sight but you
your bleach-blonde hair and that shit-eating grin
still razzing.

everyone's lost a balloon in the sky
but to think you toured your band
secretly searching for my face in the crowds

to think years later
the balloon that slipped away and disappeared
came back.

Goldstream Trestle

Swimming at Thetis

I saw your long body across the lake
copper scales of sunlight
glistened on your back

time remade me as a tree; a willow
chopped down, reaching for you
like years ago

I stared at your wet reflection
until it faded. you were so clearly next to me
your soft mouth
my trembling lips–
what would it be like to kiss?

the moon's face was slippery with yolk
my legs like canoes, rocking in the wake.
I wanted to make love

after your swim
after you walked right through me
through the trees
shrugging off your skin
with that famous grin

like years ago.

Through your Eyes (a seagull murmurs)

calm today on a salt beach
your face beams in the breakwater

I'm too far from home to celebrate you
my heart mewls like a gull
trapped in my chest

my skin forgets the sea
as I have forgotten its purpose
I lean to the water's edge
whistle till my lips are raw

I make my own footprints in your photo.
I can walk around the island now
almost touch

bring the ache in the weather
send the cemetery. I like to run in the rain
I like to walk on dead people
looking down urns for nettle, bone
a throat slit by its own sword

my hands have been still so long
I can't tell what they hold; kelp cocoons me
a whale laps me into the sea

I am those numb limbs, that girl
washed up on the beach
I feel the thrill of blood surge
part of me living again

the dull clink in my ribs
that little heart, not quite fifteen
and you calling back to me.

I LEFT THE ISLAND BEHIND with my brother and sisters in the spring of 1988, just a few months before my fifteenth birthday. Our mother wanted to get the hell out of Langford. Her marijuana pal with his caterpillar moustache had moved to Toronto and told her it was a great place to live and raise kids, that it was booming with jobs, opportunity and good schools; what an asshole.

Mom left us with family and took off for Toronto to get things sorted for our new life; she got a job and an apartment on the 11th floor of a building, and a month or so later, she sent us the plane tickets.

I have a sharp memory about much of my island life but leaving our house behind is a blur. I don't remember what happened to my pets, my piano or my books, I don't recall much aside from the box of things I could take with me. A few childhood ornaments, a mold of my crooked teeth, some school photos of my friends, a teddy bear, some Metallica posters and a miniature teacup that I won at a birthday party for eating my cake the fastest. That's it, the house might as well have burned to the ground as we drove away.

It's Hard to Stay so Far Away

I want to come home
but I'm afraid the fall will be waiting

I'll see you in green fields
your eyes lost in mine

and all the roads back
will be so far away.

Give me a Home

I've accepted being a woman who lives
mostly alone, my thoughts are alone entirely
and rot is my neighbour whose dog is barking.

I could leave this place, retire in pacific standard time
find solitude in an old book in a public house
under a warm drippy sky, desiring things like rain
and fish and fog.

do you get it? I see myself somewhere for the first time
leaning westward to the place of starting again; the coast
of promise, a mysterious cure.

I fall to dreaming, to scrounging, desiring friends
and better weather as this godawful sun lowers–
I want to face the mountains, consider what has passed
and what is coming.

It feels strange to live so far away, to raise a child
nowhere near the sea, unlike their mother
where her young mouth arrived.
Is it strange to want to be back in that wet world?
to reinvent the romance of cliffs or just sit
and watch the ships rise?

strange to be reminded of being a girl
who was never alone; who was young and wondering
about a time that should have never arrived.

It's an unfinished story with memories that I mark
as my own; questions I will answer on my own
for now, quietly alone
like the next-door neighbour in a small village
whose dog is barking.

A Langford Mollycoddle

your words wrapped me
in a flannel cocoon, a red-checked
embrace holding two thin branches

your tongue, tugging at my core
as you lurched drunk over the laneway
our bloodied roots reaching
beneath a scarred, earthen shield.

your voice, so soft like injun sun
burning fog off the lagoon

and your mouth, making a mess of me
like a fruit explosion muffin
still hot from the oven
devoured on a cold and lonely morning.

ASIDE FROM THE CRAZY FAMILY across the street with their nine, fucked-up mustard eating children of whom terrorized me with stories of the boogeyman, strange surgical procedures and creepy renditions of playing house, Sooke, (my childhood home until Grade 6), was a relatively innocent place to live.

Memories are reminiscent of paintings or fables, like the rope my father noosed from the giant cedar that became our swing, how it puts me in mind of a French oil painting, "The Happy Accidents of the Swing", which is both delightful and appropriate because for many years that swing swooped us up into the forest, over the fairy's cottage and beyond the knoll, into whatever danger that may have lurked in the woods that day.

My siblings and I were thrust into many curious and spooky adventures that had us dodging bogs and skunk cabbage, experimenting with quicksand or tugging the old man's beard to catch our balance before falling into the bubbling mud below— or worse, into the terrifying grasp of the howling banshees! We'd race out of the forest in a panic, yet still able to grab a fistful of salmonberries on the way out.

I can still smell that island mud, full of frogs and moist decay, so black and sticky as tar. And oh, the creatures, the trails of slugs and snails across my bedroom window, the invasion of wood bugs that gathered in the corners of my room, and of course the insidious pig that hid under my bed at night with its razor-sharp teeth. It took many years for me to realise what it really was, though I never looked under the bed; not once, not ever.

Condiments 1976

my brother was one year older
and when he was turning four
I spread mustard on a bun
prepared with a wiener, boiled
and made only of pork

my mother and my father
celebrated his birthday wearing
party hats and a grimace
flashing mouthfuls of soggy dogs
between songs.

I dodged houseplants
when my mother fell through
the storm-glass the night before
and she told me it was just ketchup
on her sleeve

and I was small
sat with a wiener on my plate
wondering why I was the only kid
who liked mustard.

How I Became a Vegan

the slog of memory through this rolling fog
reminds me of the split-pea soup
you forced down my doily-gagged hole

a dreaded landscape of sackcloth and ashes
whenever I winced at the dinner menu;
the picky child wears no disguise.

the blow dislodged a lump in my throat
as you dusted the dog-ears
of your favourite cookbook

I sulked through a field of daisies
crushing their tongues with galoshes
and stuffing their heads in my pockets.

my cheeks drained at the squawk
of that koklass pheasant when your hands
levelled her gullet to the block

storm-clouds strewed my reflection
with each plop of rain, time ticking backward
as I hid in the rabbit hole

you waited in the galley; lips stained
with chokecherry,
penance slumped over the ax.

Sunday Dinner

my morning search for the missing
bunnies led me to a shoebox
next to the woodpile; a coffin cradling
their slick black, furry backs.

I poked gently at a soft crumpled spine
when a hiss of air escaped its still-
warm bones.

I carried them to the carport where Father
was lurking, his wild hair and pitchfork teeth
blowing the fluff like dandelion; blue ribbons
and good luck dangled from his fingers.

I held dinner to my chest.

WE CAMPED IN A CIRCUS TENT during the summers in Bamberton; it was brown and yellow striped, big enough for six men and it smelled of mildew. I'd undo the giant zipper and a waft of old must would blast me in the face. I loved it, such a Nanny's basement kind of feeling, reminding me of ghosts and her treasure chest full of crinolines and shoes for dress-up. Everything smelled mouldy, and that of all things, is the scent of childhood bliss that never escapes my mind.

Camping in mid-summer was my favourite time; when the arbutus tree would surrender its golden leaves, those crisp yellow potato chips that crunched under foot and its reddish bark that peeled like sticks of warm cinnamon. The handsome crow with his slick black plumes perched on the drinking fountain, tipping his hat as if he recognised my face each year. The hemlock was also a good friend, guiding me with its feathery, down-sweeping branches; its short, smooth needles and unassuming cones, not pompous or aggressive like those nasty pines. And let us not forget the drowning; all the near-drowning by my brother's affectionate hand; all the times he slam-dunked my head in the ocean, how he held me under until I was choking on seawater, my overly concerned parents basking in the sun, looking away…

That's how it was when we grew up; it was a classic storybook childhood full of wonder and fantasy yet laced with all the dark things that make it traditionally Grimm.

That said, a very unsavory event caused everything to come crashing down. Instead of Bamberton and days at the beach, it was flying flowerpots and broken windows, savagely destroyed rose gardens, tears dripping into bowls of cereal, empty bottles of booze and endless nights of Laura Branigan— my parents were getting a divorce.

Bamberton

On why I Hate Bob Seger

I'm in a shit mood
listening to my mother scream.

she just tripped on her bell bottoms
and crashed through the front window

I won't bother to check on her
Joe and aunt Sarah will help her to bed

I fucking hate Fire Lake. I'm seven years old
and still crying over it

Boar

when I was a little girl
a wild pig lived under my bed

and when the dark began to grunt
I spied through slits in my fingers
counting tusks in the silver
moonlit cracks

oh how it was quiet
as it crushed my bones and pressed its kiss
into the tiny mouth of night

how it was black
as I tore the live wires from its back
its tongue lashing a lamb
basting on the spit.

Gravy and Potatoes in a Big Brown Pot

my childhood bed rolled down the aisle
of the antique fair; the braided girl
tucked into dust-caked diaries.

I rubbed memory into my cheek
as I nuzzled the fuzz of a man's coat sleeve;
a few old ghosts ran from their footprints.

I railed for the things I wanted; Nan's old crinoline
and my peter rabbit cookbook that burned
in one of the fires. I wondered about the patty pan
wept over the jam tarts.

memories dropped deep into an armchair
deep into the canvas of rainstorms and potato eaters
as I stood corrected by the family yardstick.

parasols and gumboot foliage scattered in the foyer
as the scent of mould drifted into my nostrils;
phantasms of summer, dressed like a war-time secret
as we lolled over vinyl records in Nan's basement.

my fingers dragged across the loosely framed art.
how ugly it all was; the sailing ships, the old maids
yellowed like those hideous ducks.

I bumped into Bunnykins dancing around my porridge
the fat little German kids sulking on the shelf
and that weird little naked boy yanking his penis

his gaze on my shoe buckle
slowly weaving up my tights.

Title borrowed from a recipe in the Peter Rabbit Cookery Book

Barbara Ann

been so long since I spoke to my dad
that when I heard this song playing on the radio
I burst into tears.

sounds just like him
making me feel like a little girl
with love in my heart.

well, that's over.

Heart of the Anemone

When I was a young girl living on the west coast, I wandered the beach in my gumboots with my blue, polka dot umbrella looking for treasures that decorated the shoreline. The sky was most sullen, and the sea, soda-bottle green as I collected sand dollars, shells and driftwood while the foghorn haunted the shores.

What I enjoyed most were the tide-pools; those tiny ecosystems full of magical creatures; miniature mermaids and the shipwreck of barnacles, a kaleidoscopic creation offered by the waves crashing far enough to pool in the rock's lonely crevices.

It was the tide pools where I discovered the sea urchin and I became deeply fascinated with them. Those vibrant pink and purple hues, their softness and grace as its splendorous feelers danced in the mirror of sky; so carefree, so open and innocent.

On one uncertain day, grown sour by my parent's injustice, I went to the tide-pools and crouched down to the surface, and I suppose out of anger and cruel curiosity, I poked the sea urchin with my stick. I was startled by how quickly it closed on itself, how rejected and hard surfaced it became, and I waited and waited for it to open again, but it never did.

Not to be confused with the spikes of the fierce and more formidable urchin, my beautiful pink anemone with her exquisite rhythmic limbs unbeknownst hungered and full of sting if slighted—

O' that tender heart, open and unquestioning as my own, and for man to be so careless as to injure her sweet core! With such curse these memories come; the dolour and regret that I too, have been cruel, and though these hurts come with griefs I cannot name, a newly acquired armour hath not surprise, for any unwise man with careless stick or stupid tongue, shall not survive her sting and sword.

I went to Langford once
and a seven-year-old smoking a cigarette
told me to go fuck myself.

LANGFORD WAS ROUGH. It's difficult to imagine that a town on the same little island could be so different from another, only 20 minutes away. But it was.

I was eleven years old when we moved from Sooke, and I was terrified. The kids at Ruth King Elementary were a totally different animal and they intimidated me. They seemed a lot older and more experienced; they were tough, they said words like shit and fuck, they listened to this new thing called heavy metal and some of them even smoked cigarettes. Boys followed me around, taunting and teasing, some wiped snot on my coat, some pulled my hair, some tried to kiss me and some played dogpile which was just a disguise for dry humping.

One time, and only once, did I cry in the cloakroom when no one was looking, but as frightening as it was adjusting to the harsh change in pace and attitude, it didn't take long for me to fit it in. It's probably safe to say that Langford officially ruined my innocence by my twelfth birthday. And I loved it; with the onset of puberty and the divorce of my parents, the rebellious vibe of Langford was just what I needed.

Skirt Mountain 1986

I was thirteen, I wore braces
I stole change for slurpees

I met a boy, he gave me nicknames
he wrote me love notes
I rode around on his handlebars

we lied to our parents, we hiked up a mountain
we started a fire, we had Old Dutch potato chips
we were full of wonder, we were coming of age

he wanted skirt
he was waiting for my cherry
I started my period, I didn't want to tell him
I didn't know how to tell him.

his parents tracked us, they crashed our camp
they said it was too dangerous.

I was relieved.
I didn't have to tell him
I didn't have to tell him I wasn't ready.

the parents said we could camp at home
they made their way down the mountain
they told him to pee on the fire
they told me to come and stay

we pitched a tent in his backyard
the parents looked away.

Langford Girls

got the wild in them; defiant eyes
thick with warpaint, lust flows out of them
like wasps

they got guts in them, hard-
wired hearts; pain straightens their spine
it holds them up like streetlamps

they wonder how they'll ever be beautiful
chewing skin around their fingernails
sticky with the taste of half-sucked sweets

they wonder how they'll ever be graceful
riding their bikes with grazed knees
legs kicked out, fist in the air.

Lucky

It's called Indian's brew out on the coast. we'd hitch with Murph
to Duncan and poor Paulie would wet himself after a good day
of drinking; sometimes I'd wake up warm with his stream of urine
down my legs.

Junior and me chased shrooms in the back of Murph's van.
I sat on his lap with a flat of cans as I stared into the dark spaces
in his smile; his hands snuck down my bubble-gum jeans.

I slept in a tepee at girl-guide camp; cold floor flooding
while we lapped Lucky suds with the boys from the reserve
undies hung from the flagpole–

I wasn't fifteen sucking foam off them short rounds.

The Devil Comes with a Rubber Snake

my childhood friends were a rare breed
they made up things like Anarchy and Satan

they eluded the cops with blue fizz
they put bombs in paper planes
it was dawn of the dead vice-principal

they waged war on the orthodox
and dragged the cross of Jesus
through the streets of Langford

sometimes I think I left just in time
other times I'm just pissed
because I wanted to be famous too.

Biological Tomfoolery

I was learning stuff in biology class
with my friend McColl. he was my lab partner.
he was always late, but he was always smiling

a mouthful of chiclets and cheek-folds
extending to his ears, his smile was so wide
his eyes narrowed to small slits—
sometimes I wondered how he could see at all.

we did labs on cells and sex organs
because the curriculum said kids in grade nine
were mature enough.

I said, "hey McColl, why don't you drive your
seminal vesicle to school sometime?"

he said, "cuz my boot's still stuck in your womb"

we laughed so hard our teacher sent us to the hall
which was fine because we had to dissect eyeballs next
and we were far too young to be taking a good
hard look at ourselves.

Witty's Beach

he drove a pinto he had Whiplash
in the tape deck he wore a red-checked sweater
there was mischief up his sleeve
he had twenty-four cans of O'Keefe

he took me to the beach
he said it made a good drinking place
we walked along the waterline, he was draped in leather
he overdressed for the weather
there was a Trojan horse in his trousers

we snuck inside a cove, we were scalloped by shadows
we were long black shapes making out
in the shallows, the moon dripped
its bright bulb of yolk, the tide stole our beer
we were oblivious
love barely beside our footsteps
skin-deep in water.

The Brown Bus

It was Stu's idea, he had tricks in him
he was t r i c k y

we walked to the chink store
I know it's racist it's just what we called it
we didn't know

so it was a store
owned by an asian guy
he sold us smokes we were twelve
we liked the maroon pack
they smelled like spices whatever

we went for ex-lax, the chocolate kind
with its rich and creamy
delicious disguise

we had our eye on this kid
he wasn't a skid we were just foolin'
what else was there to do

we called him over, he was small you know
smaller than me
he looked up to us whatever
kids are terrible

he looked at the candy
Stu was diverting, it was working
my face was hurting, he took it like a baby

his eyes were big and soft
softest I'd ever known
it was cruel, he rode the city bus to school
took the shitty bus home.

Teen Dope Hypnosis

my bro was a total stoner
clay-baked in the chicken coop
his body all underwater without the water
and man, if he wasn't slow enough already

he kept his stash in a tin of mints
in a lizard in a skull
in the fort full of paraphernalia
he liked getting me high, he gave me a super-toke
I choked; I went deaf
I was dancing with dirty laundry

he said it's the tobacco, let's hot-knife instead
but mom lost her shit
when all her knives wound up red
some were burnt and black
and hidden in the shed

she said it smells like skunk
when I butter my toast
what happened to my coke?
some bottomless bottle for funneling tokes?

we did acid; we waited and waited
so we just went to bed
then boom! eyes wide as spiders
and marshmallows in our heads
sock puppets and cider
and fingers long as wizards
and Raggedy Ann she put a spell on me

she staggered up the sidewalk
she was smoking colts she'd been
drinking at the Westwind she
blew donuts in my face
they were powdered sugar opiate-laced

we hitched downtown, my heart was racing
kaleidoscopic purple city
facing parliament

a pauper came fiddling it was New Year's Eve
rats rose from the gutters
like coins in a drain, they were tarnished green
and some were gold
I picked them all for my pockets

it started to rain
the clock chimed we had rockets
in our brain, there were holes everywhere

and it's like we're still there
he's still got a perma-smile, he's still fucking slow
I'm yelling for the green stuff
he just leans over, offers me a puff.

Joe's Spaghetti

some kids had to eat dinner
before going out to play

not our chaotic, busted-up family
but some kids did, like Joe.

we were at Holly's having a séance
he arrived late but he was ready
he was smiling, his belly was full

we smoked a fatty
sipped hooch from the bottle
we played Paranoid on the ghetto blaster

we summoned demons by candlelight
my arms were floating
Joe's belly was groaning
his face went white

he broke the spell
lurched upstairs and out the door
it was still daylight, I was surprised
he was lying on the ground
I had to squint my eyes

I knelt on the grass
there was dinner on his clothes
he said I'm fine, go inside

but I gave him the hose
poor Joe with spaghetti
coming out his nose.

Tootie Ramsey

as if I named him after some ten-year-old black girl
who wore braces and roller skates
what was I thinking?

it wasn't until we were older that he questioned
the source of his nickname; we must have reminisced
about the facts of life.

I reminded him of Tootie's bubbly gossip
the snooty Blair and Natalie too, the atypical sex-kitten
(chubby girls were easy in the 80's).

and there we were, walking home from school
the eldest of his three younger sisters
teasing him with a girly name
as I smacked his legs with a licorice whip;
he could've shoo'd me away with his breath
but we were too busy giggling.

looking back, I should've called him Jo
but she was a bit of a dick
and I still like the way Ramsey rolls.

he's miles away, but I awoke at 5am this morning
thinking of this big man called Tootie
crackin' gum on roller skates
and I burst out laughing.

for my brother, Paul

Ghetto Spencer Townhouse 1986

Mr. Mallett

was a hitler wannabe
he had a thick
broom-like mustache
he'd spit things like soot and poo
splitting hairs
and yardsticks too

he was the mount saint helen
of tantrums, he was a ripe tomato
ready to burst. he had a alter ego
with a goblin's thirst

he was the willem dafoe
of heinous headmasters
the king cartel
of detention hell
he'd say pink isn't well
he's ah, back at the hotel

he was lord of delusions
with a weapon in his name
he punished the fools
who failed at his game

those kids he killed and ate
through his infamous
80's reign.

Barbie's Ho Aerobics

I hated gym class, I wasn't athletic
I was more of a thinker.

we had to do aerobics because that goddamn
smoking hot jane fonda went VHS viral
with her new workout

my gym teacher was an exhibitionist
strutting around like a flamingo in her hot-
pink body suit, trim with fashionable
elastic waistband and matching leg warmers.
her legs went on forever
stretched like bridge cables arching over clouds
tits bursting out the bodice.

she'd play that song by olivia newton john
she'd sing:

let me hear your body talk
it's getting hard this holding back
if you know what I mean

I'd just stand there and watch
as she worked herself into a sweat; face flushed
squirting water on her breasts
that wet stain between her thighs
so neon you could see it glowing from the yard

all the boys were hard
especially when she'd leave the gym
and 'swish-swish' down the hall.

Hot-Boxing vs Hot-Knifing

hot-boxer: "I need a light"
 "dude I'm holding it to your face"

hot-knifer: "harsh"

Mike Dick Cooks Chicken Cacciatore

he tied back his albino hair
and strapped on a stiff white apron

home economics was a vulnerable place
for a teenage boy
so many knives, so many girls
all that circumspection…

then
prime the hen
dust it in flour
find the wet spot

nob of butter
sprig of thyme
a slug of wine

I can't remember if he cooked anything else
in that class, but that day I sucked his fingers
salt-dry, leaving a scant pile of splinters
on his plate

and no one forgets a dish like that.

Man from the Westwind

after a hard day of drinking
he still comes 'round for that foul slut

she pours 'em stiff
ole whiskey dick takes her straight up

the juke mumbles something
money for nothing
as she grips the softness in his thighs

he strikes his fist down
tosses a twenty for her dreams
not worth much.

Champs

I'll have a barley sandwich
a porn star on the ceiling

bring me fog on the river
a chaser of hooch
I want to get wrecked
with a white Russian

I don't want to be rescued
I don't want the moon

I want to shove my head under
whatever's on tap and keep chugging
till you look like someone
I want to f—

My Little Pony Fiasco

my twentieth birthday was epic
I spent it with Jess, she was my homegirl
she had a case of Lucky
we planned to get wrecked

we smoked a doobie in the yard
we headed to the bar
we took the pony, not the horse the car

we hit the Westwind
it was a pub everyone knows that
it was my first
not the pub, the pony
it was red it was the worst

I got drunk and tossed the keys
Jess tucked them in her sleeve
she gave me coin for the payphone
I called a cab that's how I got home

I slept in my clothes
dad woke me with the crows
said I reeked like ale but he always had bail
he carried a spare he said let's go
let's get your car I don't want it towed

I saddled up the pony
it smelled like circus, like lions and peanuts
I was still a bit drunk
there was junk in my teeth
there was Garbage on the stereo

I pulled up to the house
there was a car in the driveway
it was red, it was Jess, she was sitting in a pony
there was garbage on the stereo
it wasn't mine

I said what the hell, two ponies in the drive?

her eyes bulged, we burst out laughing
she jumped back in the pony
back to the pub

it was quarter to nine in the morning
there were sirens roaring
it was an accidental crime
it wasn't her fault it wasn't mine.

Heart of Langford 1995
photo courtesy of internet

I'D BEEN BACK IN ONTARIO for three years by 2002. My brother and middle sister had moved to BC's mainland, and by that time I had two children; a son who was 2 years old and a daughter, 15 months. I went out to visit them with my kids; we planned to go to the island as well to see Gram and Nan. We had a lovely visit at Beacon Hill Park while my son chased the ducks; people scowled at me and my unruly child, but I didn't give a shit.

My daughter wasn't walking yet; she spider-crawled like a side-winder through all sorts of disgusting crap, so it was bath time back at Gramma's in her nice little James Bay condo where she had her beautiful needlepoint framed on the walls, and her trinkets and china neatly displayed in curios. After the bath, my children routinely ran around naked, when my son suddenly squatted and dropped a deuce right on her spotless, white carpet. I was horrified. Our female hierarchy is cut from the cleanest, most impeccable cloth, signifying a queen somewhere in our bloodline, but Gram thought it was hilarious as she laughed heartily with her glass of sherry.

My sister and I stayed at a B&B somewhere near the Breakwater. I'll never forget driving down Dallas Road, my kids strapped in the back as we passed all the trendy joggers. We rolled down the windows and shouted at the top of our lungs, "*Victoria sucks!!!*"

Sometimes it was just easier to hate it.

The Flowers Bloom So Much Earlier Here

my lips touched the sugar and I felt sick.
the baby licks the beaters and the cat paws a sticky spill.
I'm supposed to bring the cake.

I think of your butter sandwich, the soft yellow
oozing out the sides, how you gave me the tightest hold
I ever felt in my life.

you can't put your arms around me now
you have no flesh, no skin.
my childhood feels like a boneyard
I'm forced to walk through
each time I visit; my family is missing
and all the markers are gone.

I baked a cake, but she'll find it too bright;
the ribbons are violet and the flowers are too yellow
how she must suffer the atrocity of spring.

the clouds this morning cannot compare
to how heavy my heart is; I miss you here
the sun is where you are, it's in your eyes
my God, where am I

An Easter Poem

I whisk myself to sky
with each pump of creaking swing;
memory pulls its leg through the sand
as if to keep the pebbles
skipping away my youth

they look like jellybeans
jumping the moon
and I toss them into wind's
wicker basket

a lulling yolk beams through
the cloud; its sacrificial glow
halos my lips and ears. dying lamb
cannot hear the rustle of cabbage
or the bunny licking his paws behind
the wheelbarrow.

it's an early spring to arrive
at this hollow threshold,
with old nan smiling in sheep curls
at grandad's blasphemous ramble.

the lamb on his shoulder regards me
dutifully; through spit and tallow
I'm drawn to its stillness, eyes honeyed.

wonder should I cross them
with faith and leap into the skin
of childhood where I once wept
for Jesus; hold its wounds
to the mouth of a lily
beg forgiveness for those
who gnaw the bones of Christ.

Tea with Gram

from the ceiling fan
angels came, unaware of
Gramma's broken specs.

her guests went unseen
as she poured tea, befuddled
by milk and sugar.

when the late Aunt Alice
brought birthday cake, she scowled
searching through the fog

"and for what?" she asked
of living in a sick-bed
urging me to stay

"I love you", I said
and kissed the raspberry lips
I'd known as a child.

I left her today
hoping she'll remember this;
knowing that I will.

Gramma and Jenny on Stornoway 1976
photo from family archives

Song for my Totem

on the wings of a stellar
        I hurried home to tell her
     that her ashes in the cellar
                I would save

with the dust from her estate
         I planted lilies at the gate
      my mate pressing cedar
             for her grave

called the raven from the west
        puffing lyrics from his chest
   "the psalm and the sorrow
               leave to me"

I obliged the stormy ride
        upon the mighty killer's hide
      and paddled to Tsawwassen
             with the tide

with the fog settling heavy
       raven vanished from the levee
     wading through the mist
             I had tried

and if I hadn't been so frail
      I'd have found the strength to sail
    and barrel through the gale
             at his plea

I'd have tiptoed through the trees
         with his spirit next to me
      my brother
        my totem by the sea.

Orca

blue
glass blown
pod across the wharf,
we breathe the navy breeze
bruised along the shore

red
bourbon flare
burns slow through my kin
blood harpoon slays our name
we rage upon these waves

green
ivy weeping
behind your monstrous eyes
my severed roots lie
jaded by the seaside

yellow
haloed sphere
your fins reflect a glow
my shame shaded in ghost mosaic
our past adrift with the tide.

Silver Girl

Silver girl, petals on the breeze
your song weaves a calm
softly through the trees.

Rest, silver girl
your limbs by the sea
sail the skies of sherry
leave the rye for me.

Stay, silver girl
in my arms no longer
I'll find your face reflecting
in the sparrow's quiet waters
your smile embroidered on my sleeve.

*for Gramma Joyce's Memorial Service
Hatley Cemetery, 2009*

Dear Arbutus

how I admire your slender limbs
the way your skin peels away
in delicate red coil.

how exquisite your poise, your subtle
vulnerability, so innocent and unassuming
like the child I once was; raw, unscathed flesh
exposed so simply to the world

a tiny world on a tiny island
marked with tiny footsteps.

how I've missed you
how I've longed for your shade
to umbrella the edge of my sadness.

will you still be here when I return?
will you surrender your golden leaves
along the forest floor and make it my bed?

I just want to lie down in your beauty.
I just want to hold onto this moment
for even in death, you bear my sweet youth.

Root of the Matter

that place I left unattended
like a tree dense with idle branches
unbefriended leaves, the memories planted
my dream

where the sticky kiss of youth
forces its way through as my roots
tunnel deep in the ground.

where I pull and pull until they come away
in my hands; a slow tremble under my flesh
that feels like the strength of love

a love I wish I could tend, your body
covering mine like a clump of moss
that sinks into the earth and disappears.

Sheep

the dream tastes of lust
or river water; a pale flask of longing
cleft to the brim

flesh tilled between rain-logged lips
claws thrust into forelock, no lonesome cries
no stone unturned.

as pretend as I nestle in its coat-sleeves
the dream is my shepherd, leading me home
in the wet dripping distance.

I scrape back the milky fog of its breath
ankle-dig through the gorge
of unmolested flowers.

I joggle the flask for one last drink
before herding the ghost
to its carcass

the wool blows over,
it's wearing nothing but wolves—

everything in me
leaks out like a cracked jug
on the fencepost.

Spectres of Us

it's days like these
so quiet and unassuming
that above my dreaming sea
and through the windows
of the sky, the rains come
and you're suspended in drops
on my wet and blurry gaze.

If I were a Siren

I'd glide like a water-
snake along your body
feel you shiver

I'd sing an octave of laughter
and watch you oscillate
in the sun

I'd wring your heart out
until you leaked the clear liquid
of an ocean; open your ribs like a boat
and sail you, miles deep.

I Don't Give a Shit about your Weather

seasons pass without
roots or branches
absence rips me
of splendor

my heart abides
but some of it hides
and some of it rots
under the snow

your island song
warbles in the wildflowers
makes me long
for warmer climate

spins me into a miserable
little planet, heavy
with the cold

somewhere
you've never been.

LANGFORD HAD ITS OWN DRESS CODE: tight jeans, (washed after every wear to ensure snugness), high top sneakers, denim or leather jacket, and an adorable 80's mullet…but the most important article was the mac jacket (or Langford dinner jacket/Langford tuxedo); a plaid flannel that was to be worn worked-in and faded, (burn the fuzz off with a lighter) and cut to fit underneath the jacket. It was the Swiss army knife of clothing, serving as a coat, a blanket, a disguise for illegal substances, a wound dressing kit and a burglar assistant.

There were a few colours to choose from: red and black, green and black, and the renegade hybrid purple and red version, which was insipid. Red was for black tie affairs, green was for bush parties—wait… bush parties *were* black tie affairs, never mind. At any rate, if you were hanging out at the Spencer tennis courts with the shrubs or anywhere else in Langford, you were wearing one; even the girls. Though girls also wore bubble-gum jeans, slouch socks and sweatshirts with wolves on them, and if you were really cool, you had a black tasseled leather purse hanging off your shoulder.

I was too poor to have a leather purse with tassels and I never had a mac jacket of my own until I went back for the reunion last summer, but it was a girly kind. I mean, I'm kind of a lady now…
sometimes.

A Langford Reunion

(because your face is a special occasion and I don't want to feel under-dressed)

I know we missed out
on our knife-throwing adolescence

and my heart shrunk cold as a gizzard
on the day I had to leave

but I will drink to show you
I can still be warm
and when we kiss
I'll purse my lips like a codfish
to show you I remember the sea

and tomorrow
I'll wear my Langford dinner jacket
to show you I'm still me.

.

It's Weird Being a Teenager in your Forties

we saw each other again for the first time
wide-eyed and curious, clutched arm in arm
we crashed the party and ubered home
too drunk to perform.

we awoke skin to skin
in a blanket on the floor, it was cold
my clothes were all over the road—

we hiked down to the swimming hole
he didn't take my hand
it's like I never left
like there was no need to coddle
he knew my feet would remember

I was nervous.
not about the cliff or the climb
or how cold the water was
but how much older my body was.
he was busy not noticing, like a schoolboy
like he was starstruck and shying away

he jumped in the river
so, I jumped in too.

the cold snapped the halo of my hangover
it totally seized my lungs
he held me a moment, kissed my cheek
it was wet, hard
I loved it, I could feel it

like salmon spawning
like a trout leaping from the river

I peeled away from my bikini
I tried to conceal my breasts, he loved it
like we were thirteen and budding
like it was our first time

he draped his towel around me
we touched shoulder to shoulder
he was blushing, we hardly said a word.

we cracked a beer, I was drunk in three sips
like we were too young to be drinking
but too old for hair of the dog

and I don't know how we became so close
after so long; I don't know if it was real
or if it was wrong, but we were breathing
our hearts were beating, we had something
we both wanted

and believe me
I wanted him right then and there
we were so clearly young
so clearly in love

and happy doing nothing about it.

How am I to Know?

sometimes the island's vengeful sun
threatens to crush my eyelids
and the smoke from the fire
fills my black lung

but it's temporary
I know the suffering won't last.

and it's funny really, until I came home
I believed I was long buried

but I've visited the dead
and I feel very much alive.

though it's debatable
because it's much hotter here
than I remember.

Fishing at Langford Lake

he doesn't say much but he's good
with a line and he knows what he wants
when he baits the hook.

he got a nibble but he couldn't keep it
he didn't skin it, gut it or eat it.

doesn't meant he didn't want it.
catch and release is a tricky sport.

the lake will slowly evaporate
and so will we
doesn't mean there isn't love there.

doesn't mean I didn't want to kiss him,
let him ride below the crupper
while I gripe for trout in a peculiar river.

Time Travel

we were together for just a moment.
we were fourteen
and we were forty;
it was morning, it was silent stifling
nearly departed.

night has fallen here
and things are so much harder.
I fell asleep through dinner
and served the eggs too early.

yesterday was years ago
and I'm waking up in the wrong bed.
I missed your birthday
and I'm probably too old for you now.

tell me
if I lose these hours
you will show me what I miss?
if I continue to write poems
into the soft lines of your ears
will you still hear me?

if you close your eyes
will I disappear?

See You in Another Twenty Years

that's what he said to me when I repacked
my suitcase; I didn't have words
just dipped my finger in a bottle of whiskey
and ran it along his lower lip

when he asked for a souvenir, I gave him my kiss
a flame from an age-old fire
that he sucked until my mouth blistered.

Considering the Soil for my Funeral

a thin wind flirts with the trees
as I sit near a sun-baked grave; it teases the leaves
into dancing, brittle arms break into song.

I try to recant my baptism, but I'm distracted
by the quarrel of blackbirds and the rustle of snakes
in the sticks, the waking ghost whirring
mistaken for smoke.

I try to remember the seasons; the rain
the sun and sea; the reason why I'm here.
I touch things so I can learn again
but the pain seeps through the bandage
like water drawn from the soil.

I let it come in, but I'm not interested in explanations.
I'm fine with the truth, I don't need to hear it;
the mountains here hang heavy enough for everyone.

I don't want to die, but if I do, bury me here;
this place is heavenly, there is so much ash
it gets in my eyes but I'm not crying

though I do feel the tug
as my flesh and fingers sink closer to my roots
closer to the soil than ever the sky.

Even Salmon can Find their Way Home

she spurns at the obstacle of leaving; twenty years
reeled from her birthright having bit down hard
on the sharp hook of fate, yet still she thrashes in the arms
of gravity, breaks free and beats her way upstream.

she glitters like coins in the sunlight, dances
to the drag of tide as she swishes her tail in the riverbed;
eel-like slithering through rock and crevice
before she hurls herself against the current.

so full of life, bleeding invisibly beneath every
lift of gill, no hunger or fear as she breaks through
the red wall, her jaw unhinged gnawing water
as she curls deathward.

she's too weak to breathe yet she continues
to swim against time; wielding her blood-rusted weapon
as she makes her way back to her ancestral bed.

IT WAS A SHOCK LEAVING THE ISLAND; like I woke up one morning and I was dropped from the sky onto a gigantic slab of concrete; it was a hard land.

Ontario was a foreign place with too many people and too many sounds. The air was different, it smelled like tin and exhaust; the altitude and attitudes were different. Water was different; the bread, the butter, the milk, everything was wrong... it was steel instead of wood, it was grey instead of green; bodies of water brought death and waste instead of kelp and seashells, smokestacks littered the horizon instead of freightliners. It was monochromatic shades of depression, there were ashes falling from the sky...

My aunt drove us to the airport when that solemn day arrived. I was hungover from a 26er of Silent Sam thinking I'd be making my final night in Langford a memorable one, but instead, I awoke in a stranger's house with no recollection of the night's events; I didn't know how I got there or what happened to my friends, and I only had one shoe.

I spent a good amount of time throwing up in the bathtub once I made it back to my aunt's house; I remember looking over the edge of the tub at my vomit thinking I saw worms crawling in it. I didn't know what was happening to me; all I knew was that I was going somewhere far away, and I needed shoes.

Four bewildered kids arrived at Pearson International Airport in April 1988 wearing t-shirts and sneakers; no jackets were needed as it was springtime on the island, but it was winter in Toronto. I learned new words like windchill and flurry and Tim Hortons, but I didn't understand what they meant, and I didn't want to. We took a taxi with our mother to a city called Clarkson, just an hour south of Toronto. It was bizarre not having not seen her for so long, she looked different; taller, thinner, her hair was cut short and she was excited and hurried. I didn't share her feelings; I closed my eyes in the back seat during the drive; numb, hungover, tucked in a ball trying to keep warm.

Ghost Girl

remember the house, hiding under green
tongues of moss, the drive lined with plums bulging
vodka-soaked juicy fruit?

and above, chicken coop and wine jugs.
the devil's banner, the Iron Maiden of young love
parting lips; her first, bitter and sweet all at once.

and what lies there still? the old piano
dozing in the parlor, its teeth yellowed with age
a nightgown dangling in the attic like a body
a crooked photograph of a girl fading?

wonder is about these things
when the wind opens a window to the past;
her heavy-metal hair, the cherries lining her casket—
have they withered, have they soured?
whose dream is this anyway?

under what ocean, in which house fire
in what memory, hour, year
were her cries countless?

which life carried her innocence
those bones built in her
that little body, flesh-filled full of love?

in what existence did she wake
and feel the fell of darkness, her heart blood-
brimmed with curse?

the fire was intended, but the house
still stands, I can see it through the window
the kids are still drunk, waving goodbye
and that girl is calling back.

An Island Confessional

when the mind weighs eternal
one must call upon their constant
to guide them through timeless regret.

I look to the sky this white day of winter
and wait for the rain.

Pebbles

what I come back for
are the memories, the young footprints
the redolent scent of love

the stories we tell over and over
until they become a shape of their own

worn soft like rocks
thrown in the tumult of the ocean
eroding like old bones
until they become smaller and smaller

like tiny pebbles that fit in the hollow
of my hand.

Painting Rain

in memory of us
a single lung breathing

our skin reflects in mirrors
the brush to love's waking wall

the sky's beautiful blue baboon
blowing bubbles
a hot-air balloon heart-shaped
and floating away

a buttercup dissolving on the tongue
lighting up under your chin

shades of pink
blushing watermelon
the kiss we tasted summer

white swept to a peak
and snowdrops between us
a storm committed to memory
repeated silently under breath

and the rain, a canvas
draped over your mouth

lady slipper, blue flax
tricycle red...

Blackberries

I love picking blackberries;
reaching my arms high in the briars
as I fill the bucket for jam-pots

mid-August brambles scratching at my heels
as dewdrops and spider-thread
glisten in the morning light.

tiny buds burst into pink majesties
as their wild, rambling habits
spread down either side of the lane
the sea rolls gently at the end of it
spraying the thicket with its salty, white mist.

a canopy of plump black nubs
heave above like carpenter ants
juicy and ripe with flies
bees nuzzling their fat bellies.

I could stay here all day wearing a crown of thorns
with their sticky thimbles perched
on the tips of my fingers

I could eat them one-by-one
or shove them in my mouth by the handful
leaving stains on my tongue
and my palms smeared with the sweet
blood of summer.

Root of Desire

no matter how strong my limbs
when life digs so deeply around me
even as I cup the roots in my hands
trying to keep what remains intact

no matter how thin my skin
having bore no acceptance of snow
or how urgent the need may be
to replant myself for good

there is still a suffering
a slight withering, a terrible hesitation
when the roots are always torn
between logic and desire.

Home, 1198 Goldstream Ave

THE LAST HOUSE OF MY CHILDHOOD sat across from Langford Lake on Goldstream Avenue. It was old and spooky with a dirt basement and old newspapers buried under the crawlspace. There was a missing persons story from 50 years prior and I was obsessed with it. I went hunting for clues, discovering a creepy old doll in the forest up the hill and a baby's shoe partially buried under the porch. I was convinced someone murdered a child at my house, but my mother wouldn't listen, she said my imagination was too wild. She was probably right.

The driveway was a 90-degree angle with yellow plum trees lining the way, we also had walnut trees, but who cares, nobody likes walnuts. One summer my brother and I picked a bunch of plums off the trees, soaked them in vodka, ate it all, got sick, and never touched another plum again.

Behind the house and up the hill sat an old abandoned chicken coop; a hideaway clad with Black Sabbath and Judas Priest posters, beakers and hoses stolen from the science room at school, a stuffed crocodile, hash pipes, zigzags, old carafes of wine, a ghetto blaster and a few skull ashtrays. It was *'the fort'*, and we spent more time up there than in the house.

We made a campsite further up the hill in the deep woods where my brother and I pitched tents, stored food in coolers that we snuck out of the kitchen, built shelves with tree branches to hold supplies, and a roaring campfire properly set with stones all around; we were expert wilderness kids. As it was, we were preparing for a big bush party and all of Langford was invited. At least thirty kids showed up that night, but we got busted because the look-out guy at the bottom of the driveway who was directing traffic to the path next door, got bored and bailed on us. The rest of the kids went up the hill behind the house where they were spied by my little sisters through the back window. I can hear them now *"Woah, look at all those kids, can we go too?"*

That was the end of it, all we heard ringing through the forest was *"IT'S YOUR MOM!!!!"* and like a village full of frightened mice, everyone scattered into the dark, including me. My brother just stood there pie-eyed stoking the fire, slowly uttering *"Wuttt?"*

1198 Goldstream is my Life Path Number

stumbling home under the map of Orion
was easy, but in the cusp of coming of age
something changed the direction of things

stars stopped leading me home
and all the signs suddenly
        sloped
                downhill

I don't know much about numerology
but if you whittle it down, that house was number one.

I was never number one but I did things my way.
I dug my heels in the ground and fought
feeling the same betrayal as you
when I watered down the vodka.

I may have lost the battle, but part of me
prevailed; it waits at the top of the driveway

sometimes still
sometimes swaying

like a soldier on a hill, waving no flag
like a column of blood biding time.

Ghost Girl II

I memorized her like a song I loved in high school,
one I knew perfectly out of tune with my head tilted
to one side.

it was as if I crawled inside her mouth, through her dark
passageways where all her wounds were hidden.
I watched them bleed a little before sewing them shut
but I knew they'd reopen like any loose stitch in skin.

it wasn't just pain, there was tenderness and love in her
in her blood and bones and I swear it was all for me

I took it all in, so far in, so strangely inside me; it travelled
along my spine pressing soft, untouched muscles
that hissed with relief; her lungs rising and falling
with the tide, my heart eroding

but it was her soul I remember most, alive and raucous
like the music of a hundred dead people dancing
perfectly in tune.

My Nostalgic Disease

as I leaf through the obituaries
in the relationship section of my diary
I notice the sky's thick textures of torment
and a rumbling of chords progressing in the distance

and I wonder why I bear upon such sufferance
with the haunting symphony of a raincloud?

why must these funerals for life's left-behind moments
flood my seemingly impervious face?
has my heart not narrowed far more than it has opened?

a crow lands on my windowsill; his beseeching caw
interrupts my contemplation; such a lovely narcissist
admiring his oil-slick feathers regardless how close
the storm comes.

the onslaught of rain releases every elemental fragrance
cooked in the soil; every molecule of memory
I've dragged across the ocean.

my thoughts fall homeward to a misty sheet of fog
a ghost cloaking the mouth of the lagoon;
that heavy heart overwhelmed with mist
its lusty echo tumbling from the mountains.

there are tea roses and the sea, and a body
I want to sleep next to; a gymnasium floor
and the rubber souls of youth squeaking underfoot—
thunderhead above and love's throaty respiration.

I peek out my window; the rain has stopped.
here come the villages of mice, the snakes in the grass
the sheep in the meadow the cows in the corn...
you get the picture. the leaves are down
I've had enough.

I can smell the petrichor rising from the earth;
my youth, a decomposed, flowerless material.

do not despair, these are just moments
of my nostalgic disease, and while I wish
to bury these tales of longing, without them
I would have no memory, no love, no poetry.

Lagoon

where we made the fire
in the summertime

driftwood and briar
scattered on the shoreline

the phantom thorn of young love
thrust in my side.

your hands travelled
the length of my spine
like migratory birds

fleeting,
as ships sailed and the sun
wore down.

was it worth the hour
to soothe our torn hearts?

we've wandered far
since then; those birds
are long gone now.

This is the Fall

when love's shoulders were buff
grey cliffs to hang from
on some cold, mist-shrouded day

and the rain
bored with longing's predictable face
sails a boat down the rivulets formed in my cheeks.

when the scent of fermented wet leather
as I abide this bastard weather
floods me like a broken water main.

this is nostalgia. let us watch it arrive
the way our whiskey revisits through the vomit
burning our nostrils.

when love wore hideous green briefs
and still expected a blowjob behind the school bus
as if he were some self-appointed superhero

when every girl blew out the knees of her acid-
wash jeans just to please him;
see his chest puffed out like a cock,
his hands on his hips; see his invisible cape
flapping in the wind.

this is nineteen eighty-eight
in case you hadn't noticed, when safe sex was taboo
and the token condom in a teenager's purse
was just cool-girl insignia.

I earned my badge in a chicken coop
with love's tender hand to hold me; like all those
orphan-annies with sperm
shoved high in their young vaginas.

though no small, drunken body was fruitful
at times I think they wished for it; a clean husk
of heart to mend that sluggish vein of grief
carving demons out into the night—

seems no matter how far away I go
I still find them here, though I no longer have room
to keep them. I close their casket of misfortune
and toss it back in the dirt.

this is the fall. let us watch it depart
like the ghost of my love
who will not come out to say goodbye,
nor will I linger in case it changes its mind.

Slowpoke

I miss your fingers lingering in my hair
tickling my bed-
side manner with your genial
absurdities.

I want your tongue pushed back
into the ass-end of my heart
plugging the hole of my stinking
childhood loneliness

your metaphorical rope
still strung around my neck
strangles my heavy load of indecision.

no sleep of mine can manifest
without a dream of you
yet still I sit under this eastern sun
so very slow to come home.

These Bones

weighed down by so many suitcases
by the flesh of babies
I have carried; these bones

encased in the armour of tiny vessels
wading through mud and river
for the blood-red roots
that lead me back. tired bones

lugged from house to house
unpacked and reassembled
to brace the falling roof

and goddamn the splinters
the needy mouths sucking marrow
the hollow clang of windchimes
from bones I've exposed

bones I've hidden and some
I've cried over, bones I've buckled under
not praying, just on my knees in the dirt

these bones made of soldiers
waiting to carry the body home,
these bones

they haven't broken yet.

Sometimes Stars are Assholes

I followed the stars when I lived out west
and found they were the same in the east.

and though it may sound cliché, I prayed to them
every night I was away, to send you a message
only you'd understand, to lead me home
with my heart in your hands

but that dumb bunch of stars
they never gave a damn,
they told me to go to hell

so I pray now to an empty sky
because I know damn well
it doesn't matter what I try

I know you can feel me in some small way
don't need some dumb bunch of stars
to tell you I miss you everyday.

If You Forget Me

know that my heart was once derelict
broken and worthless
when I left you

because as it was, in the past
your love meant all to me
it ran deep and it bled.

I've grown tired now;
the thought of returning
has consumed me, ravenous
that I have become too weak
to continue this old habit

so I'm asking you, one last time
to remind me
where I come from

to sit in the wind with its salty sting
and tell me how it feels;
to sit on the shores where I have roots
and tell me nothing's missing

but if you forget
know this

to live a life apart from you
bearing such love, such hopeful things
even if there is no real intention

is odd; it is impossible
without you.

A Langford Love Poem

Lord of the last to leave
my ghetto-decked disaster, I've returned to you
still addicted.

you run through my veins like gutter dirt
shouldering my burdens on the edge
of the night; your streets slick with rain
and drenched leather, cushioning my bones
through every stumble home

star-crossed with teenage hope
cigarette pressed between my lips
pretending I was older—
that's when I fell for you
far down those calamitous roads
where your wet drip of promise
licked my eyes clean

and all that I lost
first loves, first kisses, my nerves
my virtue, you claimed as your own, and I knew
I knew I could never leave you.

let me never lose sight of your pale
bruise of youth, let me cross your streets
daringly, I'll dip my toes in your fountain spew
of truth, I'll forgive your fancy progress
your sobering plot and treason

I'll give myself to you, ever after
for you are the lust in my blood
the lead in my spine;
you are the curse that haunts my heart
with this dark love.

On Longing

I have dreams sometimes
reminiscent things that harbour
all my longing

like the sea
the ships and the fog
a fish wrapped in yesterday's news
or a photograph of me looking much younger
leaping drunk in the river; my heart
having found its love

and though these dreams
sometimes make me tired, it's the melancholy
that leaves me most breathless.

Hatley House

I hadn't been home in years; that summer was a piping
hot pie with burnt crust, no cherried pink mulch
no soft peach or plum.

the house was entombed with golden brush, the gardener
weed-whacking rock-tile. the length of grass, brown-baked
in the earth; an overgrown wheat field prickling my feet.

Nan was at the window scowling; a tiny lady
with an acerbic slur and a robust chuckle that followed;
she wasn't fond of the caretaker.

Gram was rosy-cheeked in a vibrant blue gown
with a glass of sherry in her hand; she was cheerful despite the curl
of that famous raspberry frown.

Uncle Dave asked what the hell took me so long; Auntie Sheila
sat with a grin in a leather vest across from him.

David swirled his fingers in the fishpond; nothing survived
the drought, but he had that same dreamy look we all had
when we were children in that house.

I beamed with amusement; I wasn't very prepared.
I should've watered the grass or planted hydrangeas
or fired that piss-ant gardener, and I apologised for
not bringing sandwiches and gin

but they just laughed and said:

*"don't fuss with a home where nobody lives
we've been dead a long time you know".*

Salty Leave

I never belonged anywhere; that rusty old anchor
renounced my bones years ago, the pain
still winched between the wind and my breast
as I squint toward the sky

a pale-yellow scarf drapes over the lagoon
as ribbons of smoke curl around my shoulders.
clouds, like ships full of old tragedies
drift in the haze.

freightliners haunt the horizon; some appear
to be smoldering under the thick cloak of smog
others simply disappear.

I listen to quarreling waves lap the coastline
as squawking gulls scrap over the dregs of my past;
some old ghosts still stranded in the backwash.

I can't get enough; there is never enough.
I take one last breath under the dying bulb
of sunset, like a paper doll crumpled in the fire
with only a few moments left to burn.

House on Hillside

here is the bony floor
the wartime rug, foot-worn and thin;
here was a former door
where all the children walked in.

here are the merry faces
and the ghost who reads the news;
here are the curious places
of timeworn cloaks and shoes.

here's the man who was lost at war
sitting in this velvet armchair
and above the bed in goth decor
hangs a woman framed with a stony glare.

It's been so long since we gathered here
when the old were near and I was young
before the goldfish disappeared
and the house collapsed its weary lungs.

and now, no diamond stucco gleams
no dirty thirties dress up dreams
no orange and yellow spotted fins
no biscuits stored in British tins

yet at night when I visit here walking
I can see the house beyond the trees;
sometimes I see the dead folks talking
and they just smile and wave at me.

Piece of Shit Birds

only real seagulls
live by the sea.

The rest are imposters
fed by land-lovers
who steal your french fries
at lakes during holidays.

You can take the girl
out of Langford
but you can't take Langford
out of the girl.

Joe's Sandwich

I'll bet he made it with the tunes cranked.
with ordinary, run-of-the-mill
Fairway multigrain bread, and stuffed it
with oh-so-mega eggs; probably two
maybe three if he was playing hockey that day.

and I'll bet that sandwich was delicious
because there was likely a squig of sriracha
and a dash of Robert Plant in that motherfucker.

Jenny's Boat

I've let things slip.
I've become some forty-year-old shrimp boat
hanging onto an old name like Jenny
hanging onto a glimpse, a rundown town.

I look out the window to an island of people
always people arriving

but I am leaving
and the body that holds me together
is barely breathing

seawater surrounds me as I sink to the weight
of this leaving disease.
little beads of sound well in my throat.

a vibration pulls me back
a love that rallies softly around me as I sit here
contemplating.

I see things now; this boat, tied
to a strangled post of disconnection

I'm going to have to change that.

A Lake is not an Ocean

some days I can't tell
if I'm slipping away
or if I'm just stuck
behind this transparent
sheet of time, treading
in the strange mist
on a lake that pretends
to be a sea.

How Soon is Now?

soon is home
and home is when at last
I can surrender the sound
of how lonely I feel

soon I'll have snowdrops without the snow
and your lips riding up my thighs
like cherry blossom tattoos

that's all I need
as long as I'm arriving.

but not today
and not tomorrow

for I'll be busy grieving
the day's squalor
or scrounging for a suitcase
large enough to hold
all these promises

I'm not fading or despairing
but my heart, having lost you long ago
still aches with afflictions
and I still need you anytime I want

which is now

when home is full of endless distances
and I'm forced to choose
between the rock and the hard place
of my not yet but soon.

Why We Moved Away

I wore thick blue bars of eyeshadow
I was riding in cars with boys

I was behaving badly
my brother was worse
the kids were all on dope
I spilled the rum and coke

I cut my sisters' hair
I told them Santa wasn't real

we were walking the streets
on the edge of a knife
the house was haunted
the cats had lice.

that's why we moved away.
now do you understand?

Ode to the Olde Country

I was there just to get high, to fall in love
to learn how to fly.

days on tip-toes down at the bluffs
a frolic by the broken train tracks.
the long-haired boys smoking dope
and the hollers from the drunk girls

they all said they'll be getting out
just as soon as they can
but I thought they were crazy
it was a beautiful place
I didn't want to say goodbye

folks said I was too young to stay behind
and life went by with our own set of troubles
but love, I was crazy to say goodbye

I lost everything under that Olde Country sky.

*My Langford theme song
inspired by Kings of Leon's Talahina Sky*

Langford Girl 1987
photo from family archives

Diary of a Langford Girl

I think at last
I know where to call home

at last my spine opens
to the right book
where the words, like footprints
look like my own

pages made of flesh
bone encased stories that at last

crack open.

I awoke this morning
and thought I smelled the ocean
but it was just a dead crab
I stuffed in my pocket
and forgot about.

About the Author

Jennifer has been writing since she could hold a pencil, capturing moments in poetry, short stories and years of journal writing. She has written upward of 500 poems, with themes often encompassing matters of the heart and life's array of experiences, showcasing an innate ability to express the human condition in uniquely emotive ways. Some of her work has been published in various magazines, including The Blue Island Review and I-70 Review in Kansas USA.

Her trip home to Victoria BC in August 2018 inspired her to write this book as her first published, collective theme.

Jennifer was born and raised in Victoria BC, but she has lived in Ontario for over 20 years. Residing in Orillia, a small town not much different than old Langford, she makes her home in a gingerbread house with her two teenagers, two small dogs, a cat, three rats and a rogue skunk that lives under the shed. She hopes to move back to the island as soon as possible.

All proceeds go to the moving fund.

Made in the USA
Monee, IL
30 June 2021